Buffy the Vampire Slayer™

ADULT COLORING BOOK

With Illustrations by
PABLO CHURIN
NEWSHA GHASEMI
REBEKAH ISAACS
GEORGES JEANTY
YISHAN LI
FERNANDO MELEK
KARL MOLINE
STEVE MORRIS
FACUNDO PERCIO

DARK HORSE BOOKS

Into every generation a Slayer is born:
one girl in all the world, a Chosen One.

She alone will wield the strength and
skill to fight the vampires, demons, and
the forces of darkness.

To stop the spread of their evil and the
swell of their number.

She is the Slayer.

Buffy: Does it ever get easy?

Giles: You mean life?

Buffy: Yeah. Does it get easy?

Giles: What do you want me to say?

Buffy: Lie to me.

Giles: Yes, it's terribly simple. The good guys are always stalwart and true, the bad guys are easily distinguished by their pointy horns or black hats, and, uh, we always defeat them and save the day. No one ever dies, and everybody lives happily ever after.

Buffy: Liar.

—Season 2, "Lie to Me"

Cordelia: Oh, look, it's the Three Musketeers.

Buffy: Was that an insult?

Xander: Kinda lacked punch.

Willow: The Three Musketeers were cool.

Cordelia: I see your point.

Xander: I woulda gone with Stooges.

Cordelia: Well, I just meant that you guys always hang out together. So, did you guys fight any demons this summer?

Willow: Uh, yes! Our own personal demons.

Xander: Uh, such as—as—as lust and, uh, thrift!

Buffy: I would have to go with Stooges also.

—Season 2, "When She Was Bad"

SUNNYDALE
HIGH SCHOOL

Willow: The one boy who truly liked me, and he's a demon robot. What does that say about me?

Buffy: That doesn't say anything about you.

Willow: I really thought I was really falling—

Buffy: Hey, did you forget? The one boy I've had the hots for since I moved here turned out to be a vampire.

Xander: Right, and the teacher I had a crush on? Giant praying mantis.

Willow: That's true.

Xander: Yeah, that's life on the Hellmouth.

Buffy: Let's face it. None of us are ever gonna have a happy, normal relationship.

Xander: We're doomed!

Buffy and Willow: Yeah!

—Season 1, "I Robot, You Jane"

BRONZE

Giles: You have responsibilities that other girls do not.

Buffy: Oh! I know this one! "Slaying entails certain sacrifices, blah blah biddy blah, I'm so stuffy, give me a scone."

Giles: It's as if you know me.

—Season 2, "Inca Mummy Girl"

Angel: I knew this was gonna happen.

Buffy: What? What do you think is happening?

Angel: You're sixteen years old. I'm two hundred and forty-one.

Buffy: I've done the math.

Angel: You don't know what you're doing. You don't know what you want.

Buffy: Oh. No, I—I think I do. I want out of this conversation.

Angel: Listen, if we date, you and I both know one thing's going to lead to another.

Buffy: One thing already has led to another. You think it's a little late to be reading me a warning label?

Angel: I'm just trying to protect you. This could get out of control.

Buffy: Isn't that the way it's supposed to be?

Angel: This isn't some fairy tale. When I kiss you, you don't wake up from a deep sleep and live happily ever after.

Buffy: No. When you kiss me, I want to die.

—Season 2, "Reptile Boy"

Angel: Well, there's gotta be some way around it.

Giles: Listen, some prophecies are—are a bit dodgy. They're—they're mutable. Buffy herself has—has thwarted them time and time again, but this is the Codex. There is nothing in it that does not come to pass.

Angel: Then you're reading it wrong.

Giles: I wish to God I were. But it's very plain. Tomorrow night Buffy will face the Master, and she will die.

—Season 1, "Prophecy Girl"

Drusilla: Do you love my insides? The parts you can't see?

Spike: Eyeballs to entrails, my sweet.

—Season 2, "Halloween"

Drusilla
and
Spike
SJM 16

Buffy: I wish we could be regular kids.

Angel: Yeah. I'll never be a kid.

Buffy: Okay, then a regular kid and her cradle-robbing, creature-of-the-night boyfriend.

—Season 2, "What's my Line?, Part 1"

EN
YDAY
SNOW
WORLD
FUN
TIME

Cordelia: Eww, what does this do?

Giles: What?

Cordelia: What does this do?

Giles: Uh, it, uh, extracts vital organs to replenish its own mutating cells.

Cordelia: Wow. What does this one do?

Giles: Um, i-it elongates its mouth to, uh, engulf its victim's head with its incisors.

Cordelia: Ouch. Wait, what does this one do?

Giles: It asks endless questions of those with whom it's supposed to be working so that nothing is getting done.

Cordelia: Boy, there's a demon for everything.

—Season 2, "Killed by Death"

Buffy: It's just . . . You're never gonna get noticed if you keep hiding! You're missing the whole point of Halloween.

Willow: Free candy?

Buffy: It's come-as-you-aren't night! The perfect chance for a girl to get sexy and wild, with no repercussions.

Willow: Oh, I don't get wild. Wild on me equals spaz.

—Season 2, "Halloween"

Harmony: I'm glad your mom stopped working at the drive-through long enough to dress you . . . Oh, that reminds me. Did you see Jennifer's backpack? It is *so* trying—

Cordelia: Harmony, shut up! Do you know what you are, Harmony? You're a sheep.

Harmony: I'm not a sheep.

Cordelia: You're a sheep. All you do is what everyone else does, just so you can say you did it first! And here I am scrambling for your approval when I'm cooler than you 'cause I'm *not* a sheep. I do what I wanna do, and I wear what I wanna wear. And you know what? I'll date whoever the hell I wanna date . . . No matter how lame he is.

—Season 2, "Bewitched, Bothered and Bewildered"

"We're going to destroy the world. Want to come?"
—Drusilla, Season 2, "Innocence"

Buffy: How did you find me here?

Angel: If I was blind, I would see you.

Buffy: Stay with me.

Angel: Forever. That's the whole point. I'll never leave. Not even if you kill me.

—Season 3, "Anne"

Faith: All men are beasts, Buffy.

Buffy: Okay, I was hoping to not get that cynical till I was at least forty.

Faith: It's not cynical. I mean, it's realistic. Every guy from . . . Manimal down to Mr. "I Love *The English Patient*" has beast in him. And I don't care how sensitive they act. They're all still just in it for the chase.

—Season 3, "Beauty and the Beasts"

Angel: You can't imagine the price for true evil.

Faith: Yeah? I hope evil takes MasterCard.

—Season 3, "Consequences"

Xander: But . . . it's just that it's bugging me . . . this "cool" thing. I mean, what is it? How do you get it? Who doesn't have it? And who decides who doesn't have it? What is the essence of "cool"?

Oz: Not sure.

Xander: I mean you, yourself, Oz, are considered more or less cool. Why is that?

Oz: Am I?

Xander: Is it about the talking? You know, the way you tend to express yourself in short, noncommittal phrases?

Oz: Could be.

Xander: No, you're in a band! That's like a business-class ticket to cool with complimentary mojo after takeoff. I gotta learn an instrument. Is it hard to play guitar?

Oz: Not the way I play it.

Xander: Okay, but on the other hand: Eighth grade. I'm takin' the flugelhorn and gettin' zero trim. So the whole instrument thing could be a mislead. But ya need a thing. One thing nobody else has. What do I have?

Oz: An exciting new obsession, which I feel makes you very special.

—Season 3, "The Zeppo"

ROUTE
US
66

Oz: You mean . . . you'd still . . .

Willow: Well, I like you. You're nice, and you're funny, and you don't smoke. Yeah, okay, werewolf, but that's not all the time. I mean, three days out of the month, I'm not much fun to be around either.

Oz: You are quite the human.

Willow: So, I'd still, if you'd still.

Oz: I'd still. I'd very still!

Willow: Okay. No biting, though.

Oz: Agreed.

—Season 2, "Phases"

"There's more than one way to skin a cat. And I happen to know that's factually true."

—Mayor Wilkins, Season 3, "Enemies"

MAYOR
RICHARD

Faith: There's only supposed to be one. Maybe that's why you and I can never get along. We're not supposed to exist together.

Buffy: Also, you went evil and were killing people.

Faith: Good point. Also a factor.

Buffy: But you're right. I mean, like . . . I guess everyone's alone, but . . . being a Slayer? There's a burden we can't share.

Faith: And no one else can feel it . . . Thank God we're hot chicks with superpowers.

Buffy: Takes the edge off.

Faith: Comforting.

—Season 7, "End of Days"

Oz: Guys. Take a moment to deal with this. We survived.

Buffy: It was a hell of a battle.

Oz: Not the battle. High school.
—Season 3, "Graduation Day, Part 2"

ratulat
ss of 1999
s!

Giles: Who are the gentlemen? They are fairy-tale monsters. What do they want? Hearts. They come to a town. They steal all the voices so no one can scream. Then . . . They need seven, they have at least two.

Xander: How do we kill them?!

Giles: In the tales no sword can kill them. But the princess screamed once . . . and they all died . . . Only a real human voice . . .

Buffy: How do I get my voice back??

—Season 4, "Hush"

Tara: Even when I'm at my worst . . . you always make me feel special . . . How do you do that?

Willow: Magic.

—Season 5, "Family"

Buffy: Honey, we need to talk about the invitations. Now, do you wanna be William the Bloody, or just Spike? 'Cause either way it's gonna look majorly weird.

Spike: Whereas the name Buffy gives it that touch of classic elegance.

Buffy: What's wrong with Buffy?

—Season 4, "Something Blue"

"I have no speech. No name. I live in the action of death, the blood cry, the penetrating wound. I am destruction. Absolute . . . Alone."

—Tara (speaking for the First Slayer), Season 4, "Restless"

Joyce: Dawn . . . She's not mine, is she?

Buffy: No.

Joyce: She's . . . She does belong to us, though.

Buffy: Yes, she does.

Joyce: And she's important . . . to the world. Precious. As precious as you are to me . . . Then we have to take care of her. Buffy, promise me. If anything happens, if I don't come through this—

Buffy: Mom—

Joyce: No, listen to me. No matter what she is, she still feels like my daughter. I have to know that you'll take care of her, that you'll keep her safe, that you'll love her like I love you.

Buffy: I promise.

—Season 5, "Listening to Fear"

Buffy: So Giles and I worked out a whole schedule around school, a block of time every day just to focus on my new Slayer training.

Willow: That's a work ethic! Buffy, you're developing a work ethic!

Buffy: Oh no, do they make an ointment for that?

Willow: People gotta respect a solid work ethic.

Buffy: So . . . I won't be taking drama with you.

Willow: What? You have to, you promised!

Buffy: Well, I know, but Giles says that it just—

Willow: The hell with Giles!

Giles: I can hear you, Willow.

—Season 5, "Real Me"

Anya: Hey . . . Hey! HEY! *HEY!!!*

Giles: Anya, your heys are startling the customers.

Xander: And pretty much the state!

Anya: You sold someone a Khul's amulet and a Sobekian bloodstone!

Giles: Yes, I believe I did.

Anya: Are you stupid or something?

Giles: Allow me to answer that question with a firing.

Xander: She's kidding. An, we talked about the employee-employer vocabulary no-nos. That was number five.

—Season 5, "Shadow"

Spike: I'm a vampire. I know something about evil. You're not evil.

Dawn: Maybe I'm not evil. But I don't think I can be good.

Spike: Well, I'm not good, and I'm all right.

—Season 5, "Tough Love"

Buffy: Look, I realize that every Slayer comes with an expiration mark on the package. But I want mine to be a long time from now. Like a Cheeto. If there were just a few good descriptions of what took out the other Slayers, maybe it would help me to understand my mistake, to keep it from happening again.

Giles: Yes, well, the problem is after a final battle, it's difficult to get any . . . Well, the Slayer's not . . . She's rather . . .

Buffy: It's okay to use the D-word, Giles.

Giles: Dead. And hence, not very forthcoming.

—Season 5, "Fool for Love"

Darla: I think our boys are going to fight.

Drusilla: The King of Cups expects a picnic. But this is not his birthday.

Darla: . . . Good point.

—Season 5, "Fool for Love"

Buffy: So let me get this straight. You're . . . Dracula. The guy. The Count.

Dracula: I am.

Buffy: And you're sure this isn't just some fanboy thing? Because . . . I've fought more than a couple of pimply, overweight vamps that called themselves Lestat.

Dracula: You know who I am. As I would know without question that you are Buffy Summers.

Buffy: You've heard of me?

Dracula: Naturally. You're known throughout the world.

Buffy: Naw. Really?

Dracula: Why else would I come here? For the sun? I came to meet the renowned . . . killer.

Buffy: Yeah, I prefer the term *Slayer*. You know, *killer* just sounds so . . .

Dracula: Naked?

Buffy: Like I . . . paint clowns or something. I'm the good guy, remember?

Dracula: Perhaps, but your power is rooted in darkness. You must feel it.

Buffy: No. You know what I feel? Bored.

—Season 5, "Buffy vs. Dracula"

Willow: There's a Slayer handbook?

Buffy: Wait. Handbook? What handbook? How come I don't have a handbook?

Willow: Is there a T-shirt, too? 'Cause that would be cool . . .

Giles: After meeting you, Buffy, I realized that, uh, the handbook would be of no use in your case.

Buffy: Well, what do you mean it would be of no use in my case? Wha-what's wrong with my case?

—Season 2, "What's My Line?, Part 2"

VAMPYR
SJM '16

Buffy: So you three have, what? Banded together to be pains in my ass?

Warren: We're your archnemesises . . . ses. You may have beaten us this time, Slayer, but next time . . . um . . . uh, next time . . .

Jonathan: Maybe not!

—Season 6, "Gone"

Xander: Just once I would like to run into a cult of bunny worshipers.

Anya: Great! Thank you very much for those nightmares.

—Season 5, "Shadow"

Demon: Better go, Spike. Things could get ugly.

Demon 2: It got ugly the second he walked in—him and his human.

Clem: Her skin's so tight, I don't even know how you can look at her. Ugh.

Demon: Leave your winnings and get out. And we'll forget this whole thing.

Spike: Ah, so it's a setup, innit? Squeeze a few quid out of the vamp. I'll tell you what you didn't count on: me and the bird. You wanna fight? You face the two of us.

Buffy: What? I'm not getting into a bar fight. I'll beat 'em up for information, great, but not to defend your rights to gamble for kittens . . . Which, by the way, is stupid currency.

Demon: They're delicious.

Spike: Come on, Slayer! A big fight's just what you need.

Buffy: Forget it. I'm done.

—Season 6, "Life Serial"

Riley: You want me to say I like seeing you in bed with that idiot? Or that blinding orange is your very best color? Or that that burger smell is appealing?

Buffy: You smelled the smell?

Riley: Buffy, none of that means anything. It doesn't touch you. You're still the first woman I ever loved and the strongest woman I've ever known. And, I'm not advertising this to the missus, but you're still quite the hottie.

Buffy: You know, it goes away after many bathings.

—Season 6, "As You Were"

DMP
DOUBLEMEAT PAL
DMP
Buffy Summers
DMP
EAT PALACE
EAT IS DOUBLESWEET

Xander: Figuring out how to control your magic seems a lot like hammering a nail. Well, uh, hear me out. So you're hammering, right? If you hold the end of the hammer, you have the power, but no control. It takes, like, two strokes to hit the nail in, or you could hit your thumb.

Willow: Ouch.

Xander: So you choke up. Control, but no power. It could take, like, ten strokes to knock the nail in. Power, control. It's a tradeoff.

Willow: That's actually not a bad analogy.

Xander: Thanks.

Willow: Except I'm less worried about hitting my thumb, and more worried about going all black-eyed baddie and bewitching that hammer into cracking my friends' skulls open like coconuts.

Xander: Right. Ouch.

—Season 7, "Help"

Xander: Well, the Hellmouth, the center of mystical convergence, supernatural monsters: been there.

Buffy: Little blasé there, aren't you?

Xander: I'm not worried. If there's something bad out there, we'll find, you'll slay, we'll party!

Buffy: Thanks for having confidence in me.

Xander: You da man, Buff!

—Season 1, "Nightmares"

"I'm the thing monsters have nightmares about."
—Buffy, Season 7, "Showtime"

"I say we change the rule. I say my power . . . should be our power. Tomorrow, Willow will use the essence of the Scythe to change our destiny. From now on, every girl in the world who might be a Slayer . . . will be a Slayer. Every girl who could have the power . . . will have the power. Can stand up . . . will stand up. Slayers . . . every one of us. Make your choice. Are you ready to be strong?"

—Buffy, Season 7, "Chosen"

"The hardest thing in this world . . . is to live in it.
Be brave. Live . . ."

—Buffy, Season 5, "The Gift"

SCHOOL BUS

Xander: You don't know how to kill this thing.

Buffy: I thought I might try violence.

Xander: Solid call.

—Season 2, "Killed by Death"

Angel: Buffy, you know there's still things I'm trying to figure out. There's a lot I don't understand. But I do know it's important to keep fighting. I learned that from you.

Buffy: But we never . . .

Angel: We never win.

Buffy: Not completely.

Angel: Never will. That's not why we fight. We do it because there's things worth fighting for.

—Season 3, "Gingerbread"

"If the apocalypse comes, beep me."
—Buffy, Season 1, "Never Kill a Boy on the First Date"

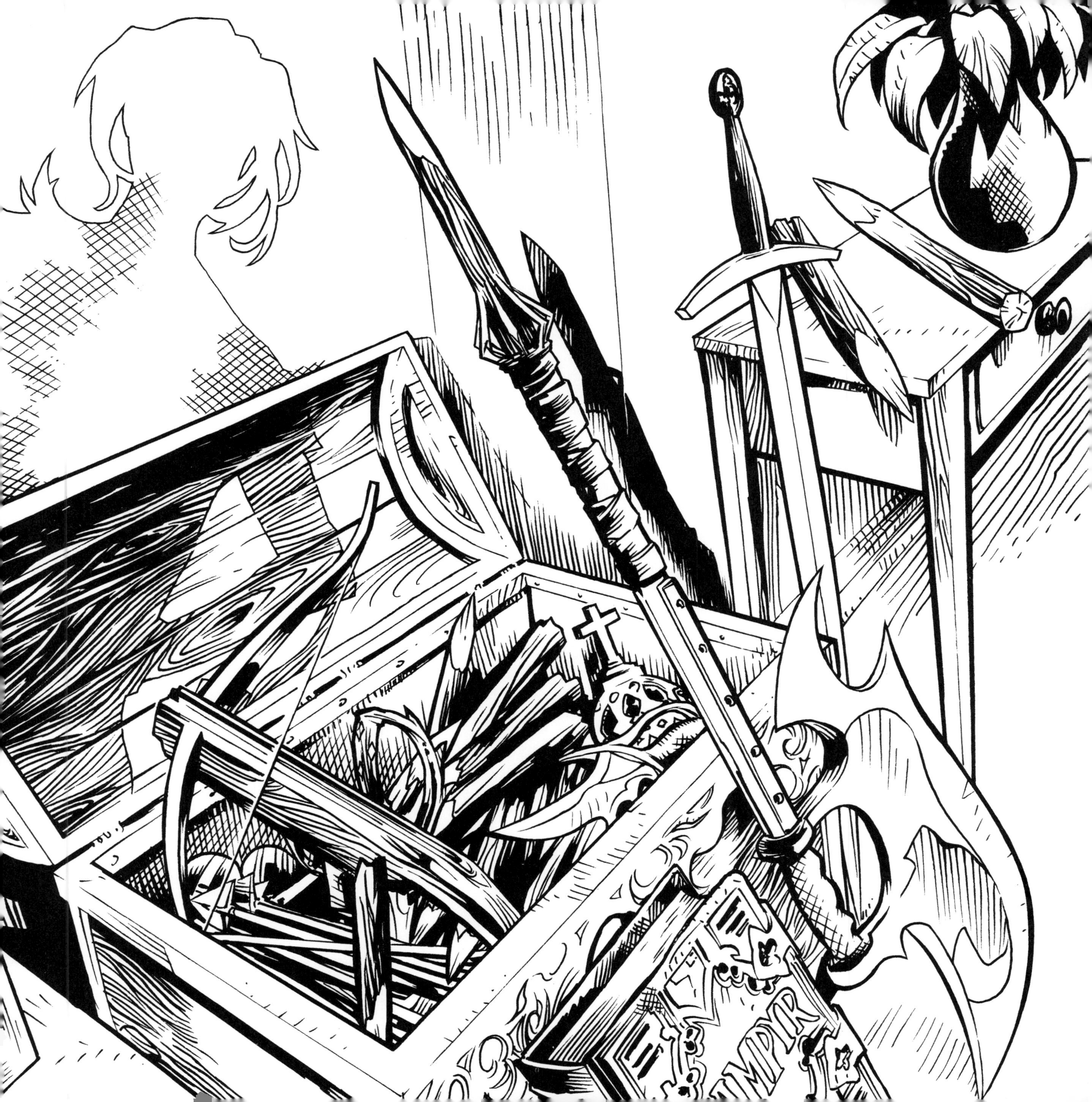

ABOUT THE ILLUSTRATORS

PABLO CHURIN *(pages 13, 25, 39, 43, 51, 57, 63, 75, 77, 85, 87)*
Pablo Churin was born in Argentina. After beginning his career as an artist for fanzines, his comics work began with a horror miniseries for Studio 407 called *Hybrid*. Some of Pablo's professional work includes *Agon* for Zenescope Entertainment, *El General San Martín* for Ovni Press, *Thief: Tales from the City* for Dark Horse Comics, *God Is Dead* for Avatar Press, and several web comics for MTJ Publishing.

NEWSHA GHASEMI *(pages 7, 33, 35, 37, 53, 59, 65, 67, 73, 79)*
Newsha Ghasemi is a freelance illustrator raised in the outskirts of Washington, DC. She has had a love of illustration since she was a kid. With caffeine-driven ambition and a disregard for a human's need for sleep, she eventually developed a career out of art and garnered experience with various notable companies, such as Gree, DeNA, Koei Tecmo, Double Take Comics, and most recently, Dark Horse Comics.

REBEKAH ISAACS *(page 45)*
Artist Rebekah Isaacs, a graduate of the Savannah College of Art and Design, got her start in comics drawing *The After Hours* for the *Twilight Zone* series of graphic novels from Walker & Co. Her first mainstream work was *Ms. Marvel* with writer Brian Reed for Marvel Comics, followed by WildStorm Comics' miniseries *DV8: Gods and Monsters* with writer Brian Wood. Rebekah entered the Buffyverse with *Angel & Faith* and *Buffy the Vampire Slayer* Season 10, and continues as series artist on *Buffy* Season 11. A native of Dahlonega, Georgia, Rebekah now lives in New York.

GEORGES JEANTY *(pages 29, 47, 81, 91)*
Serenity and *Buffy the Vampire Slayer* artist Georges Jeanty studied fine arts at Miami Dade College; the pursuit of a career in comics was a logical choice for his artistic talents. He worked for DC Comics on titles such as *Green Lantern*, *Superboy*, and *Superman*. The year 2006 brought Georges the critically acclaimed comics miniseries *The American Way*, written by screenwriter John Ridley and released through WildStorm. Georges was handpicked by Joss Whedon to become the artist on *Buffy* Season 8, the Eisner Award winner for Best New Series in 2008. He continued as the regular series artist for *Buffy the Vampire Slayer* Season 9 and recently was the artist for the series *Serenity: Firefly Class 03-K64—Leaves on the Wind*.

YISHAN LI *(pages 9, 11, 21, 23)*
Yishan Li is a professional British comic/manga artist currently living in Shanghai. She has been drawing since 1998 and has been published internationally in the US, France, Germany, Italy, and the UK, among other countries. She has worked for publishers such as Random House, Del Rey, Titan, Delcourt, DC Comics, and Dark Horse Comics. Yishan is currently the artist for the *Buffy: The High School Years* graphic novels from Dark Horse Comics.